"CODEQUEST: A KID'S ODYSSEY IN THE MAGICAL WORLD OF PROGRAMMING"

Welcome to "Undertakings in Coding: A Youngster's Involved Aide"

Hi, youthful coders! ☐

Is it safe to say that you are prepared to leave on an intriguing travel into the universe of coding? Welcome to "Experiences in Coding," your go-to direct for opening the enchanted behind PC projects, games, and activities.

Why Coding? ☐

Coding resembles recounting a mystical story to your PC. You become the creator, and the PC adheres to your directions to rejuvenate your thoughts. Whether you fantasy about making your own games, enlivened stories, or intuitive workmanship, this guide is here to assist you with moving into the brilliant universe of code.

What Comes Inside? You will learn the fundamentals of coding through engaging activities, vibrant illustrations, and engaging challenges on these pages. We'll utilize a cordial programming language called Scratch, where you'll drag and snap together vivid blocks to make your own computerized ponders.

No Experience Required! □ ⊞

Never coded? Don't worry about it! This guide was written specifically for you. We'll begin with the nuts and bolts and steadily move toward energizing activities that will

4

exhibit your freshly discovered coding superpowers.

Prepare to let your imagination run wild, solve challenging puzzles, and show off your creations to family and friends. Is it true or not that you are interested? Excited? Fantastic! We should jump into the principal section and start our coding experience together.

Prepared, set, code! □

Hello, future code geniuses! ☐

Welcome to the interesting universe of coding, where you become the head of your own high level boat. Have you anytime thought about how your main PC games or vivified films look alive? You are about to find out, so get ready to find out!

What is Coding? ☐

At its middle, coding looks like directing a PC. Imagine that you possess a enigmatic wand and that you are able to cause your computer to perform unimaginable actions by using a few extraordinary words. Whether it's making characters, making things move, or regardless, developing your own virtual world, coding is the best approach to opening this charming power.

You Are the Boss! □□

Exactly when you code, you become the manager of the PC. You get to the bottom of what's going on right away, and your computer does as you tell it. It looks like being the supervisor of your own blockbuster film or the minds behind an incredible PC game. The potential results are just probably as incredible as your imaginative psyche!

2. Why Coding Is Cooler Than Frozen Yogurt Currently, you might wonder, "Why would I want to learn how to code?" For sure,

secure in, considering the way that coding is cooler than a twofold scoop gelato on a rankling summer day! Create Your Own Games Have you ever wished you could create your own computer game? With coding, you can! From epic encounters to mind-bowing enigmas, you get to pick the norms and restore your gaming dreams.

Enliven Your Imaginative psyche

Love youngster's shows and activitys? Coding permits you to transform into an artist. Make characters dance, make talking animals, or even arrangement your vivified movies. Beyond what many would consider possible is your imaginativeness.

Do you naturally have the ability to tell stories that bring you joy? Coding licenses you to retell stories in an altogether unique way. Imagine making stories where your characters jump off the page and into the high level world you make.

Be a Tech Entertainer 🧙‍♂️

Think about coding your charmed wand in the high level space. With two or three taps and snaps, you can conjure mind blowing things. You're not just using development; You are the one who is shaping it.

All things considered, could you say you are ready to transform into a coding legend? Grab your cape and we ought to dive into the superb universe of coding! □✦⁂

Section 2: Let's program! □

Incredible! It's time to get your hands dirty, grab your digital toolbox, and let the exciting world of coding begin after you've tried your hand at it. In this part, we will investigate the nuts and bolts of coding with a fabulous device called Scratch. All in all, would you say you are prepared to get wizardry going? How about we code!

3. Setting Up Your Coding Space □□

Before we jump into the coding ponders, how about we ensure you have everything set up. Sit back and relax; Setting up your favorite game is all that is required. Follow the basic advances, and in a matter of moments, you'll be prepared to make your own computerized show-stoppers.

Step 1: Download Scratch

Make a beeline for the Scratch site (scratch.mit.edu).
Click on "Make" to enter the otherworldly universe of Scratch.
On the off chance that you haven't as of now, make your Scratch account. It's your ticket to the kingdom of coding!

Step 2: Take a Quick Tour of the Playground Explore the Scratch playground. It's where the wizardry works out!

Get familiar with the coding blocks. These vivid blocks are your instruments for making code.

4. An Overview: Your Coding Toolkit: Now that your coding space is prepared, let's examine the fundamentals of your coding toolkit. Consider it learning the ABCs of coding. We'll begin with straightforward orders and slowly move toward additional interesting difficulties.

Order Blocks: Getting Things Going

Meet the "Move," "Turn," and "Say" blocks. These resemble your enchanted spells; they get things going on the screen.

Drag and snap these blocks together to make your most memorable arrangement of directions.

Loops: Doing Things Over and over

Find out about circles, the mystery ingredient for rehashing activities.

Envision telling your PC, "Do this dance move multiple times." That is the force of circles!

Events: Setting off the Sorcery

Find the force of occasions. They're similar to the beginning button for your code.

Cause your code to answer a key press, a tick, or some other mystical occasion.

5. Fun with Scratch: Allow the Games To start! □

Now that you're outfitted with the rudiments, now is the right time to scrutinize your abilities. We'll set out on an undeniably exhilarating excursion to make your most memorable intelligent movement. Prepare to code a skipping feline, a moving sprite, or perhaps a talking outsider. The decision is yours, and the potential outcomes are huge!

Bit by bit Movement: Bouncing Ball Follow along as we collaborate to create a straightforward animation. Explore different avenues regarding various orders and perceive what they mean for the movement.
You're Turn: Redo and Play!

Presently, it's your chance to sparkle. Alter your activity, add your own style, and watch your creation become completely awake. Toward the finish of this part, you'll have your most memorable coding show-stopper. In this way, get your coding wand, and let the coding experience proceed! ☐☐

Section 3: Beginning with Coding

3. Setting Up Your Coding Jungle gym

Before we jump into the mystical universe of coding, how about we set up your coding climate. We'll utilize Scratch, a fabulous block-based programming language that makes coding as simple as stacking building blocks. Follow these moves toward get everything rolling:

Step 1: Visit the Scratch Site
Open your internet browser and go to scratch.mit.edu.

Step 2: Make a Scratch Record
Click on the "Join Scratch" button to make your Scratch account. It's your behind the stage pass to a fantastic coding experience.

Step 3: Investigate and Download Scratch

Whenever you're signed in, click on "Make" to enter the Scratch coding jungle gym. Take some time to look around the interface.

Step 4: Download Scratch Manager (Discretionary)

For a more vivid encounter, you can download the Scratch Manager. Click on "See inside" and afterward "Record" - > "Download to your PC."

Now that your coding climate is set up, how about we continue on toward the essentials of coding.

4. An Overview: Uncovering the Enchanted Blocks

Orders, Circles, and Occasions - Gracious My!

In coding, we utilize unique structure blocks to make our directions. These blocks resemble interconnecting pieces that fit together to make our code wake up. We should investigate three principal ideas: orders, circles, and occasions.

Commands: Getting Things Going

Orders are the activity blocks in coding. They instruct your PC. In Scratch, you'll find order blocks in the "Movement" and "Looks" classifications.

Example: Pushing Ahead

Drag a "when green banner clicked" block (from Occasions).
Attach a Motion "move 10 steps" block underneath it.

Loops: Doing Things Over and over
Circles resemble rehashing spells in coding. They let you accomplish something again and again. Search for the "Control" classification to find circle blocks.

Example: Drag a "forever" block from Control to Dance Party.
Add a "turn 15 degrees" block (from Movement) inside the eternity block.

Events: It's like starting a magical show when you trigger the Magic Events. They start off your code. In the "Events" category, look for event blocks.

Example: Answer a Vital Press

Drag a "when space key squeezed" block (from Occasions).
Attach a Looks "say hello" block underneath it.

Active Practice Time!
Now that you've seen a few wizardry impedes, it's your chance to play with them. Open Scratch, make another undertaking, and attempt the accompanying:

Make a Sprite that Moves:

The "move" and "when green flag clicked" blocks can be used to move a sprite across the screen.
Dance Party Circle:

Make a sprite pivot in a circle, making a dance party impact.
Memorable Story:

Utilize the "when key squeezed" block to make a sprite say something when a particular key is squeezed.
Try, have a great time, and become familiar with these essential coding ideas. You're presently headed to turning into a coding wizard! 🧙‍♂️📲✨
Part 4: Fun with Scratch: A Movement Experience! 5.1 Guided Tour: Step 1 of Coding a Simple Animation: Open Scratch and Create a New Project to Begin Your Coding Journey Open Scratch and select "Create."

Step 2: Pick a Sprite

Pick a sprite for your liveliness from the Scratch library. You can pick a person, a creature, or even an item.

Step 3: Code the Sprite's Development

Drag a "when green banner clicked" block from the Occasions class.

Add a Control category "forever" block.

Inside the "for eternity" block, utilize the "move 10 stages" block from the Movement classification.

Step 4: Add a Changing Foundation

Go to the Foundations tab and pick a foundation.

Drag a "change scenery to" block inside the "until the end of time" block.

22

Step 5: Try different things with Changing Factors
Go to the Factors class and make another variable (e.g., "speed").
Utilize the "set speed to" block to control the sprite's development.
Support trying different things with various qualities for the "speed" variable.

Step 6: Play and test!
Click the green banner to see your liveliness in real life! Explore different avenues regarding changing the speed variable to make your sprite move quicker or more slow.

6. Characters and Stories: Step 1 of Once Upon a Code: Choose a second sprite for your story to add. It very well may be a talking creature, a

cordial robot, or anything your creative mind wants.

Step 2: Code Exchange Between Characters

Drag a "when green banner clicked" block for every sprite.

Use "express" blocks from the Looks classification to make the characters talk.

Add stops between exchange utilizing "pause" blocks from the Control class.

Step 3: Change the backdrops to create a scene for your story.

Position the sprites to interface with one another.

Step 4: Recount Your Story!

Click the green banner to watch your characters become fully awake and recount their story. Try different things with various exchanges, backgrounds, and character associations.

Step 5: Reward Challenge - Add Audio effects

Investigate the Sounds class and add audio effects to improve your story. Use "play sound" blocks to make your characters' experiences significantly really energizing!

Presently, you've made an incredible movement and rejuvenated characters through code! Go ahead and investigate and change the code to make the story extraordinarily yours. The coding scene is your material — what will you make straightaway? ☐☐

Client
Part 1: Getting everything rolling
3. Setting Up:
Make sense of how for set up a straightforward coding climate (e.g., Scratch, a block-based programming language).
Incorporate download/establishment guidelines with visuals.
4. An Overview:
Present essential ideas like orders, circles, and occasions.
Give straightforward models and energize active practice.
ChatGPT
Part 1: Beginning with Coding
3. Setting Up Your Coding Jungle gym

Before we jump into the mystical universe of coding, how about we set up your coding climate. We'll utilize Scratch, a fabulous block-based programming language that makes coding as simple as stacking building blocks. Follow these moves toward get everything rolling:

Step 1: Visit the Scratch Site
Open your internet browser and go to scratch.mit.edu.

Step 2: Make a Scratch Record
Click on the "Join Scratch" button to make your Scratch account. It's your behind the stage pass to a fantastic coding experience.

Step 3: Investigate and Download Scratch

Whenever you're signed in, click on "Make" to enter the Scratch coding jungle gym. Take some time to look around the interface.

Step 4: Download Scratch Manager (Discretionary)

For a more vivid encounter, you can download the Scratch Manager. Click on "See inside" and afterward "Record" - > "Download to your PC."

Now that your coding climate is set up, how about we continue on toward the essentials of coding.

28

4. An Overview: Uncovering the Enchanted Blocks

Orders, Circles, and Occasions - Gracious My.

In coding, we utilize unique structure blocks to make our directions. These blocks resemble interconnecting pieces that fit together to make our code wake up. We should investigate three principal ideas: orders, circles, and occasions.

Commands: Getting Things Going

Orders are the activity blocks in coding. They instruct your PC. In Scratch, you'll find order blocks in the "Movement" and "Looks" classifications.

Example: Pushing Ahead

Drag a "when green banner clicked" block (from Occasions). Attach a

Motion "move 10 steps" block underneath it.

Loops: Doing Things Over and over

Circles resemble rehashing spells in coding. They let you accomplish something again and again. Search for the "Control" classification to find circle blocks.

Example: Drag a "forever" block from Control to Dance Party.
Add a "turn 15 degrees" block (from Movement) inside the eternity block.

Events: It's like starting a magical show when you trigger the Magic Events. They start off your code. In the "Events" category, look for event blocks.

Example: Answer a Vital Press

Drag a "when space key squeezed" block (from Occasions).
Attach a Looks "say hello" block underneath it.

Active Practice Time!

Now that you've seen a few wizardry impedes, it's your chance to play with them. Open Scratch, make another undertaking, and attempt the accompanying:

Make a Sprite that Moves:

The "move" and "when green flag clicked" blocks can be used to move a sprite across the screen.
Dance Party Circle:

Make a sprite pivot in a circle, making a dance party impact.

Memorable Story:

Utilize the "when key squeezed" block to make a sprite say something when a particular key is squeezed.

Try, have a great time, and become familiar with these essential coding ideas. You're presently headed to turning into a coding wizard! 🧙‍♂️✨

Section 5: 7. Coding Magic's Building Blocks Grasping Blocks: Your Coding Tool compartment □

In the immense universe of coding, consider blocks your mysterious apparatuses. Each block has an interesting power, and when consolidated, they rejuvenate your manifestations. How about we disentangle a portion of the fundamental coding blocks and find their capabilities:

Movement Blocks: Move and Section □♂□□

Move 10 Stages: Your sprite goes for a walk across the stage.

Turn 15 Degrees: Turn your sprite toward your decision.

Go to X: 50 Y: 50: Magically transport your sprite to a particular area.

Looks Blocks: Spruce Up Your Sprite □□

Make proper acquaintance: Cause your sprite to talk with a discourse bubble.

Set Outfit to "Costume2": Change your sprite's appearance immediately.

Next Outfit: Make livelinesss by exchanging between various ensembles.

Sound Blocks: Add Tunes and Impacts □□

Play Sound "yowl": Allow your sprite to sing or make fun commotions.

Limit the volume to 50%: Change the sound level of your sprite's presentation.

Control Blocks: Rule the Show □□

For eternity: Keep a code block running all the time, like a story that never ends.

On the off chance that, Else: Pursue choices in your code. " Do one thing in the event of the following: in any case, do another.

Occasions Blocks: Begin the Enchanted Show ☐☐

At the point when Green Banner Clicked: Launch your code by tapping the green banner.

At the point when Space Key Squeezed: Make actions occur when a particular key is pressed.

Factors Blocks: Your Supernatural Mixture Fixings ☐☐

Set MyVariable to 5: Variables can be used to store information and create your own secret codes.

Change MyVariable by 2: Adjust the worth of your variable during the show.

Presently, the genuine wizardry happens when you blend and match these blocks! Consolidate movement with looks, sprinkle in some sound, and presto! Your code turns into a hypnotizing exhibition.

8. Challenges: Make the most of your coding abilities! □□

Challenge 1: Sprite Express □

Make a sprite that gets across the stage, changes outfits, and plays a sound. Allow the sprite to be your express train, and the stage is its otherworldly excursion.

Challenge 2: Create a dance routine for your sprite for Dance Off. Use movement blocks to make it turn, change ensembles for style, and play an infectious tune utilizing sound blocks.

Challenge 3: Intuitive Story □□

Make an intelligent story where your sprite answers a vital press or mouse click. Use control blocks to wind around various plotlines and keep your crowd locked in.

Challenge 4: Secret Game ☐ ♂ ☐ ☐

Construct a secret game where your sprite examines a case. Use occasions to set off hints and factors to monitor the criminal investigator's advancement.

5th Challenge: Coding Conductor:

Use your sprite as the conductor to create a symphony. The costumes change in time with the music, with each motion block representing a musical note. Could you at any point form a magnum opus?

Solutions: Open the Insider facts ☐ ☐ ☐

Answers for each challenge are given toward the finish of the section. Use them as a manual for look at and upgrade your supernatural manifestations!

Part 6: Games and Movements: Opening the Wizardry! ⬜✨

9. Game Plan: Coding Undertakings Anticipate! ⬜⬜⬜

9.1 Walkthrough: Making a Basic Game

How about we set out on an astonishing excursion to make your own personal game utilizing the sorcery of coding. We'll plan an exemplary game where your sprite should discover falling items. Prepare to code your gaming work of art!

Step 1: Set the Stage

Pick a Foundation: Go to the "Sceneries" tab and select a background that suits your game, maybe a lively sky or a clamoring cityscape.

Place Your Sprite: Pick a sprite for your player (e.g., a person, creature, or spaceship) and put it on the stage.

Step 2: Code the Player's Development

At the point when Green Banner Clicked: Drag this block from the "Occasions" classification to begin your game.

Always Circle: Utilize the "until the end of time" block from the "Control" class to constantly keep the game running.

Move Player Left/Right: To move your player left or right, use "if-then" blocks with the "key pressed" condition.

Step 3: Create Falling Objects by Adding Falling Objects Copy your sprite to make falling items (e.g., natural products, stars, or raindrops).

Code Item Development: Make the falling items move descending utilizing a "until the end of time" circle and the "change y by" block.

Step 4: Getting the Articles
In the case of Contacting Player: Utilize the "in the event that" block to check assuming the falling articles contact the player sprite.

Increment Score: Add a scoring component by utilizing a variable. Increase the player's score whenever they catch an object.

Step 5: Game Over

In the case of Contacting Edge: To determine whether the falling objects reach the bottom of the screen, use the "if-then" block.

Game Over in Broadcast: Show a game over message and stop the game when the player misses an item.

Concept of Levels and Challenges Now that you have developed a straightforward game, consider ways to increase the level of difficulty as the player progresses. Present the idea of levels where the speed of falling items increments, or new sorts of articles show up. Urge players to go for the gold and conquer progressively troublesome difficulties.

10. Activity Wizardry: Making Stories Come to Life! 10.1 Teach Animation Concepts

Let's use coding to enter the magical world of animation. Liveliness resembles a spell that rejuvenates your accounts. In coding, we use ideas like casings and sprites to make entrancing movements.

Edges and Sprites Made sense of Outlines: Frames are like the pages in a flip book. Each casing addresses a second in your movement. You can switch between casings to make development and recount a unique story.

Sprites: Sprites are the characters or items in your activity. They can appear to be moving by changing their costumes.

10.2 Walkthrough: Making an Energized Story

Stage 1: Pick a Foundation

Select a Foundation: Pick a background that lays the right foundation for your energized story.

Place Characters (Sprites): Put your characters' sprites on the stage by selecting them.

Step 2: Code the Presentation

At the point when Green Banner Clicked: Begin your activity when the green banner is clicked.

Make proper acquaintance: Utilize the "express" block to present your characters and set the stage.

Step 3: Invigorate the Story

Switch Ensembles: Make movement outlines by exchanging between various outfits for your sprites.

Move Characters: Use movement blocks to move your sprites around the stage, making them show some major signs of life.

Step 4: Make a Peak
Construct Pressure: Utilize sound blocks to add thrilling music or audio effects.

Enliven a Defining moment: Make a crucial second in your story utilizing liveliness and exchange.

Step 5: Finish up the Liveliness
Wrap Up the Story: Use activity and discourse to close your story.

Stop the Video: When the animation reaches its conclusion, you can put an end to it with the "stop all" block.

Experiment and Improve In order to improve their animated stories, encourage children to experiment with various backgrounds, characters, and sound effects. They can cause various situations, present new characters, and let their creative mind roam free!

Part 7: Going Past: Make the most of your coding abilities! □□

11. Investigating More Dialects: A Coding Experience Is standing by! □□

11.1 Python with Turtle

Welcome to the intriguing universe of Python! With a friend by the name of Turtle, coding becomes a fun adventure in Python, a versatile programming language.

Beginning:
Set up Python: Visit python.org and download Python.
Open Inactive: Send off Inactive, Python's incorporated improvement climate.
Presenting Turtle: Type import turtle and let Turtle join your coding process.
Coding Fun:
Draw with Turtle: To make Turtle draw lines, use commands like turtle.forward(100).
Make Shapes: Try different things with circles to draw circles, squares, and that's just the beginning.
Consider Colors: Add tones to your drawings with orders like turtle.color("blue").

11.2 JavaScript for Youngsters

Meet JavaScript, the language that rejuvenates sites! It resembles adding sorcery spells to the web.

Beginning:

Internet Browser Control center: Open the program console (press F12 or right-click and select "Assess," then, at that point, go to the "Control center" tab).

JavaScript Enchantment: Type straightforward orders like console.log("Hello, World!") what's more, witness the sorcery.

Coding Fun:

Change Site Text: "Hello, Magic World!" uses document.body.innerHTML. to change text on a site page.

Intelligent Buttons: Cause fastens that to answer clicks with orders like

```
button.addEventListener("click",
capability() {...}).
```

Invigorate Components: Use element.style.animation to move elements on a webpage.

Assets for Additional Investigation:

Code.org: code.org offers intuitive coding illustrations for youngsters, covering Scratch, Python, and the sky is the limit from there.

Khan Foundation: Courses in coding, such as SQL and JavaScript, are available for free at khanacademy.org.

ScratchEd: scratch.mit.edu/instructors has assets for teachers, including example plans and exercises.

Mozilla Thimble: thimble.mozilla.org allows children

to make and share site pages with HTML, CSS, and JavaScript.

Turtle Designs in Python: turtle-python.com offers instructional exercises and difficulties for Python with Turtle.

12. Sharing time: Share Your Coding Show-stoppers! ⬜ ⬜⬜

12.1 Urge Children to Share:

Congratulations on your adventures in coding! Presently, it's opportunity to exhibit your coding superpowers. Urge children to impart their activities to loved ones. Here's the reason it's fundamental:

Motivate Others: Your manifestations can ignite interest and motivate others to begin coding.

Get Input: Share your undertakings to get valuable input and work on your abilities.

Observe Accomplishments: Commend the difficult work and

imagination that went into your coding magnum opuses.

12.2 Feature the Significance of Inventiveness:

Keep in mind, coding isn't just about orders and punctuation; it's a material for your innovativeness. Whether you've fabricated a game, energized a story, or coded a site, your novel touch makes it unique.

Put yourself out there: Coding is a type of self-articulation. Share your thoughts and character through your undertakings.

Problem-Solving: Coding teaches you how to solve problems and think creatively, both of which are useful skills in many different contexts.

Constant Learning: The more you code, the more you learn. Embrace difficulties and explore constantly.

Along these lines, don't be modest — share your coding process and let your imagination sparkle! □□

Presently, furnished with information about various programming dialects and the significance of sharing, you're prepared to take your coding experiences higher than ever. Continue coding and investigating the boundless conceivable outcomes! □ ⬛✦

Conclusion: Your Coding Experience Is standing by! ☐☐

13. Congratulations!

You succeeded! You have successfully completed "Adventures in Coding: A Youngster's Involved Aide." Give yourself a high-five since you've opened the mystical universe of coding. Presently, we should pause for a minute to commend your accomplishments and freshly discovered coding superpowers!

More Resources for Constant Education:
Your coding process doesn't end here. Keep the sorcery alive by investigating these extra assets:

Codecademy: codecademy.com offers intuitive coding illustrations for different programming dialects.

MIT Application Creator: appinventor.mit.edu allows you to make portable applications utilizing a visual programming language.

Raspberry Pi Undertakings: raspberrypi.org gives ventures and instructional exercises to involved learning with Raspberry Pi.

Kodable: kodable.com is a great stage for getting the hang of programming ideas through games.

Extra Tips:
Visuals and Representations:
Visual Learning: Keep in mind, words generally can't do a picture

justice. Use visuals to make coding ideas straightforward.

Represent Unique Thoughts: Complex ideas become more clear with outlines. Use visuals to separate dynamic thoughts and make them available.

Involved Exercises:
Intuitive Coding: Careful discipline brings about promising results! Remember hands-for exercises after every section to build up what you've realized.

Change and Test: Go ahead and alter existing code. Trial and error is the way to dominance. Examine the effects of changes on your creations.

Support Inventiveness:

Coding as Innovativeness: Keep in mind that coding is more than just following rules; it's a device for releasing your inventiveness.

Unconditional Difficulties: Keep the flash bursting at the seams with unassuming difficulties. Allow your creative mind to roam free and make something remarkably yours.

Parent/Instructor Area:
For the grown-ups directing our young coders:

Tips for Helping: Encouragement and small victories should be celebrated. Coding is an excursion, and each step counts.

Investigate Together: Join your youngster in coding experiences.

Learn together and find the delight of making with code.

Make a Coding Space: Set up a committed space for coding. Creativity is fueled by an inviting and motivating environment.

Keep in mind, the coding universe is tremendous and consistently extending. Continue investigating, continue to make, and in particular, partake in each snapshot of your coding experience! Happy programming!